Original title:
Flowers of Fate

Copyright © 2025 Creative Arts Management OÜ
All rights reserved.

Author: Olivia Sterling
ISBN HARDBACK: 978-1-80567-047-6
ISBN PAPERBACK: 978-1-80567-127-5

Singing the Colors of Fate

In the garden where daisies dance,
Petunias giggle, given a chance.
Roses snicker, full of glee,
While tulips plot a grand jubilee.

The sun starts to tickle the blooms,
A party erupts in colorful rooms.
Bees in tuxedos, buzzing like pros,
You can't imagine the laughs that arose.

Pansies sport hats, all tilted just so,
While sunflowers play limbo, stealing the show.
Laughter blossoms with each little breeze,
As nature sings sweetly, aiming to please.

In this realm where chuckles collide,
Fate's funny colors, bright and wide.
Join the petals in their merry chase,
For laughter's the root in this colorful space.

The Weaving of Green Threads

In a meadow where mischief is spun,
Green threads weave tales, oh what fun!
Grassy giggles and mossy mirth,
Nature's shenanigans, proving their worth.

Sage pokes fun at the bright marigold,
While clovers cheer, their hands in the fold.
Twining their stories, in tangled delight,
Every laugh shared takes flight like a kite.

Vines twirl around in a merry old way,
As daisies conspire to join in the fray.
Laughter echoes, a melodious strand,
In this green tapestry, hand in hand.

So gather your grins, and dance on the lawn,
With roots of hilarity, here we're reborn.
Threads of giggles and greens so bright,
In this weaving of joy, everything feels right.

The Chronicle of Hidden Roots

In the garden of whims, a tale unfolds,
Where daisies tell secrets, and marigolds hold.
Butterflies barter, for nectar so sweet,
While bumblebees dance, to a jitterbug beat.

Worms wear monocles, crooning with pride,
As snails race the winds, despite their slow glide.
Petunias gossip, in colors so bright,
While thorns play a game, of hide and seek night.

Cascades of Color and Fate

A daffodil chuckles, with petals so wide,
Claiming the sun, as its trusty guide.
The violets plot, with mischievous flair,
As tulips wear hats, spinning tales in the air.

The color parade, oh what a display,
With lilacs on stilts, in a cheeky ballet.
Pansies both giggle and wink at the crowd,
While daisies declare, they've never allowed.

Budding Possibilities

In a pot of dreams, seedlings hatch with glee,
Whispering wishes to the bumblebee.
Each sprout has a quirk, a secret to share,
As they lean out, hoping for sunshine and air.

The carrots conspire, below the brown dirt,
While radishes grin, in their leafy green shirt.
These green little jesters, so eager to play,
Bloom tales of mischief, in a bright, funny way.

When Time Blooms

Clock hands spin wildly, what a grand show,
As daisies keep time, with a jovial glow.
Hours drip like honey, on petals that sway,
While sunflowers giggle, 'We're here to play!'

The future's a riddle, a puzzle of cheer,
With zinnias spinning yarns, that we all hold dear.
When moments take flight, in a whimsical tune,
The garden laughs loud, in the light of the moon.

Twilight in the Vale

In the vale where shadows dance,
The daisies prance with silly chance.
A bee wears glasses, quite a sight,
Buzzing through the fading light.

The sun trips over clouds so grey,
As jolly squirrels plot their play.
They claim the acorns for a feast,
While giggling spreads, to say the least.

A Tapestry of Growth

In the garden, things arise,
With tomatoes plotting in disguise.
A cabbage jokes, "I'm quite the head!"
While peas are hanging by a thread.

The carrots laugh, their tops in curls,
As lettuce twirls in leafy swirls.
They've got a party, fun and wild,
Each plant's a little quirky child.

The Scent of Possibility

A whiff of hope in the cool breeze,
As mint leaves giggle with such ease.
The blossoms bloom, all brightly dressed,
Throwing a bash, they're clearly blessed.

The roses tease with their sharp thorns,
While daisies flaunt their pastel horns.
Together they concoct a plot,
To prank the gardener on the spot.

Budding Horizons

In a patch of dreams, the tulips sprout,
With whispers soft, they laugh about.
Each petal bright in giggles wrapped,
While sleepy bees around them zapped.

The sun plays peekaboo with grace,
As shadows join the silly race.
A painted lady makes the scene,
While blossoms wink, all fresh and green.

The Garden of Life's Choices

In the garden, choices grow,
Some are red, some are faux.
Pick the ones that make you cheer,
Avoid the prickles hiding near.

A daisy tells a joke or two,
While roses are a bit askew.
Violets whisper secrets sweet,
But watch your step, don't miss a beat.

A Symphony of Petals

Petals dance in breezy flight,
Swaying left, and then to right.
A tulip sings the blues, it seems,
While daisies giggle at our dreams.

Here comes a bunch of wildflowers,
Claiming all the sunny hours.
With every bloom, a tune they play,
In harmony from day to day.

Nature's Diverse Palette

In nature's hue, we find the jest,
A color clash that's simply blessed.
Yellow sunflowers wear a grin,
While purple pansies dive right in.

A garden gnome just shakes his head,
At marigolds who paint the bread.
A playful splash, a wink, a shout,
In every petal, joy's about!

The Bloom of Chance

Chance blooms brightly in the sun,
A poppy shouts, "Come, join the fun!"
Dandelions scatter far and wide,
Acting like they're on a ride.

A lucky clover's got a grin,
Whispering wins on a whim.
So toss your worries to the breeze,
And dance with nature, if you please!

The Language of Blossoms

In a garden of giggles, they twist and they sway,
Petals dance wildly, in a hilarious way.
Bees buzzing loudly, they tickle my ear,
As blooms trade secrets we're meant to hear.

Daisies wear sunglasses, what a curious sight,
Roses crack jokes, oh what sheer delight!
Tulips quip softly, 'We're tall for a reason,'
Who knew that plants had their own blooming season?

Garden of Serendipity

In a patch of surprise where the weeds intermingle,
I stumbled on daisies, like those who just jingle.
Sunflowers wink at the clouds up above,
This garden's a riot, like a slapstick love.

Petunias gossip while nodding in cheer,
Whimsical laughter, can you hear it so clear?
Buttercups chuckle, they've got all the moves,
Each bloom's a comedian, proving their grooves.

The Fragrance of Choices

In a forest of whimsy where choices abound,
Lilies tell stories, both silly and sound.
Violets are shy yet they blush with glee,
Deciding between a dance and a cup of sweet tea.

Carnations erupt with a raucous good time,
They argue about scents, each one a rhyme.
Freed from their pots, they're free to create,
A fragrant ruckus, oh, don't let it wait!

Echoes of the Meadow

In a meadow of laughter where daisies peek,
The grass tickles toes, it's a game that we seek.
Crickets compose a funny little tune,
While butterflies giggle, under the moon.

The wind carries chuckles, a whimsical breeze,
With blooms throwing parties beneath the large trees.
Each blossom's a joker, with petals so bright,
In this echoing joy, everything feels right.

Petals of Destiny

In a garden of choices, so bright and so bold,
A dandelion sneezed, and the universe rolled.
With whims of the wind, it danced all around,
Claiming its throne as the silliest found.

The sun made a joke about daisies in line,
Saying, 'Remember, dear tulips, it's all about shine!'
But violets snickered, 'We bloom in our shade,'
'While you all just worry how best to parade.'

Whispers in the Garden

A sunflower winked at a bashful bluebell,
'Why do you hide? You've got stories to tell!'
They giggled and swayed to the tune of a bee,
Who buzzed with delight, 'Look at you two, so free!'

Underneath the old oak, where secrets were shared,
A rose teased a thorn, 'You think you're well-pared?'
The laughter erupted among leaves in the breeze,
Causing all creatures to join in with ease.

Serendipity's Bloom

A petunia tripped on its roots, oh so spry,
It fell on a daisy, with a laugh and a sigh.
Together they tumbled, a hilarious scene,
As tulips all gasped at what could have been!

'Just wait for the harvest, we'll bloom into pies!'
Cackled the pansies, with bright, twinkling eyes.
While daisies proclaimed, 'We're the original gang!'
It's a riot in nature, where mischief can hang.

The Tapestry of Seasons

Oh, autumn's a joker, with leaves flying high,
While spring's a prankster, wearing flowers to fly.
With summer's loud laughter, the heat on its side,
Every season's a jester, we giggle and glide.

'I'm the best at confusion!' winter frosted with glee,
As snowflakes fell softly, like confetti from me.
Together they weave this ridiculous fate,
In a tapestry spun from a laugh and a wait.

A Dance of Petals and Time

In a garden of giggles and glee,
Petals waltz like they're free.
Daisies twirl under sunlight's gaze,
While roses chat in a floral haze.

Bees buzz while they strut their stuff,
Sipping nectar in a dance that's tough.
Lilies laugh, saying they're quite grand,
While tulips form a quirky band.

Breezes tickle the shy daisies,
Their giggles echo in sunny phases.
A dandelion sneezes, oh what a sight,
Sprinkling wishes that take flight!

And when the sun begins to dip,
The flowers sip tea, take a little trip.
They recount tales of petals and dreams,
In a world where nothing's as it seems.

Beacons in the Wild

In the woods, a daffodil bright,
Claims, "I'm the star of the night!"
With daisies cheering, they all agree,
That wildflowers host the best jubilee.

A sunflower boasts of its sunny height,
While clover nerds argue what's polite.
"I'm sweet! I'm lucky!" says a frazzled three,
While thistles stand guard with ridiculous glee.

Bamboo takes a break from its tall glory,
To join wildflowers in their funny story.
They huddle close, giggling and sighing,
As the world spins on, all flora relying.

And in the end, as the moon climbs high,
The blossoms whisper, "Oh my, oh my!"
With laughter echoing through starry ground,
Nature's comedy is truly profound.

The Alchemy of Blossoms

Petals huddle in a cauldron so round,
Crafting potions from sights and sounds.
Roses mix giggles with violet winks,
While marigolds plot their pinky links.

A daisy pops in with a silly grin,
"I'm the essence of fun, let's begin!"
Lavender chuckles, swirling away,
Emitting scents that lead hearts astray.

A wind gust groans, trying to meddle,
But snapdragons laugh and turn up the pedal.
Chrysanthemums boast about their new spells,
While orchids wink, casting laughter spells.

By the end of the day, a brew so stout,
Nature's magic leaves no room for doubt.
In this whimsical brew, all bloom with glee,
Creating joy, as it's meant to be!

Blooming in the Unseen

In shadows where whispers softly poke,
Mysterious flowers begin to evoke.
With giggles lurking just out of sight,
They craft strange laughter in the dead of night.

A hidden rose plays hide and seek,
With petals smirking, they hardly speak.
"Catch us if you can," they tease and taunt,
While poppies jump in like a playful vaunt.

When moonlight glows on a clover's face,
It stumbles, tripping in a clumsy pace.
Jasmine sighs and starts to sway,
As unseen flowers unleash their play.

And when dawn breaks, the fun spills wide,
With colors bursting, no need to hide.
In every bloom, a joke is spun,
In their playful world, there's always fun!

Gardens of Tomorrow

In gardens bright with sunlit cheer,
The daisies dance, not a single fear.
The tulips giggle, leaning in,
While roses gossip about their kin.

The carrots wear their leafy crowns,
While peas in pods swap silly frowns.
A garden party on the lawn,
Where snails recite bad jokes at dawn.

Bumblebees buzz, they share their tales,
Of daring flights and windy gales.
The foxgloves twirl, with flair so bold,
While sunflowers strut, their heads like gold.

As evening comes, they reminisce,
The petals laugh, none want to miss.
In bloom they find a joyful fate,
A way to dance, it's never late.

Echoes of a Hidden Path

Down winding trails where laughter leads,
The violets hum like buzzing bees.
A dandelion makes a wish for fun,
While wandering vines play hide-and-seek in the sun.

The path is dotted with silly signs,
'Beware of gnomes' and 'Check for vines!'
Each step reveals a playful twist,
As bumbles of breeze get lost in the mist.

A squirrel juggles acorns with flair,
While lilacs prank, planting seeds everywhere.
The sunbeams join a rhythmic embrace,
As petals shake in joyous race.

Echoes ring where laughter's clear,
Nature's joke, the trees all cheer.
With every turn, a tale unfolds,
And life's bright colors never grow old.

The Blooming Tomorrow

On the dawn of a brand new day,
The blooms arise in a bright ballet.
Peonies twirl with a giggling sigh,
While poppies wink as the robins fly.

Sunflowers wear their smiles wide,
While pansies boast of their colorful pride.
Each petal whispers, "Look at me!"
As morning dew joins in the spree.

A gardener trips, oh what a sight!
With watering cans, they start a fight.
Hydrangeas snicker, their shades like sun,
As laughter echoes, joy's just begun.

With every bud and every bloom,
Nature's humor banishes gloom.
In this garden, all is right,
Tomorrow sparkles, so delightfully bright.

Threads of Nature's Design

In stitches bright, the garden's spun,
As daisies craft a quilt for fun.
The violets weave their threads of cheer,
While foxgloves giggle, nothing to fear.

A bumblebee knits with steady buzz,
Forming patterns, just because.
Tulips grin with every hue,
While dandelions add a touch of blue.

The ivy climbs in playful loops,
Playing tag with the bumble groups.
Each blossom joins in threads of lore,
Weaving laughter forevermore.

As season fades and colors blend,
Nature's design, it knows no end.
With every stitch, a story's spun,
In this garden, we're all just fun!

The Secret Life of Stems

When stems wear hats, they sway with flair,
Dancing in the breeze, without a care.
Whispers in the soil, secrets they keep,
Guardians of mischief, awake or asleep.

They laugh at the sun, tickled by dew,
Plotting their pranks, between green and blue.
A wiggle here, a twist over there,
Who knew their antics would be so rare?

Roots play charades, unearthing their tricks,
A game of hide and seek with the dirt sticks.
Stems giggle softly, in the moonlight bright,
Like undercover spies in the heart of the night.

So next time you stroll through paths of delight,
Remember the stems that dance out of sight.
With laughter and cheer, they revel and shout,
In a whimsical world, where fun is about.

A Garden Written in the Stars

In a plot of dreams, where moonbeams play,
Cabbages gossip about the day.
Roses debate the best way to bloom,
While sunflowers argue who occupies room.

A comet streaks by, and tulips all cheer,
'We're twinkling tonight, it's perfectly clear!'
Daisies huddle, plotting a jest,
Their cosmic giggles are simply the best.

The marigolds sing with voices so sweet,
Dancing their waltz, can't stay in their seat.
Lily pads laugh with an echoing glee,
As starry-eyed clouds tumble from the tree.

So if you look up on a starry night,
Know blossoms and weeds are plotting delight.
Silent conspirators under the sun,
In a garden grand where laughter is spun.

When Petals Fall from the Sky

When petals rain down, the world's a show,
Dancing in circles, oh what a glow!
With umbrellas made of leaves, frogs leap ballet,
While ants form a chorus, in a grand display.

Squirrels craft hats from the colorful fall,
Giggles erupt in the garden's sprawl.
Pansies play marbles with shiny acorns,
As butterflies flutter, in joyous adorns.

Each drop brings a story, fresh and absurd,
About a brave bee who fancied a bird.
With laughter and cheer, it's quite the affair,
As petals keep tumbling through fragrant air.

So grab a good friend, let's dance in the mess,
For petals from heaven are Nature's caress.
In a world with no rules, just whimsy and fun,
When petals fall down, we're all bound to run.

In the Arms of the Verdant

In greenery's grasp, the rabbits do prance,
Joking with daisies, they leap and they dance.
Pine trees conspire with squirrels in glee,
While bushes gossip, 'Have you heard about me?'

Breezes tickle leaves, causing fits of the giggles,
Nature's own laughter, in twirls and in wiggles.
With vines wrapping tightly 'round secrets unsaid,
The trees shake their heads, 'This is quite widespread.'

The ferns host a ball, with butterflies bright,
While dewdrops peek in, to join the delight.
In the arms of the lush, where chaos is best,
Funny affairs unfold, they never do rest.

So wander on paths by the foliage thick,
You might just discover a botanical trick.
With laughter and joy, in nature's embrace,
In the arms of the verdant, we find our place.

Threads of Nature's Tale

In a garden of giggles, where daisies dance,
A squirrel in a tuxedo took a chance.
He asked a rose, with her petals so bright,
"Will you join me for tea, or just for a bite?"

Beneath the sun's grins, the weeds wore a crown,
A dandelion declared, "I won't back down!"
With a puff of his fluff, he scattered his dreams,
While a ladybug laughed at the wiggles and beams.

A sunflower yelled, "I'm taller!" quite proud,
While tulips rolled over, all laughing aloud.
The daisies just chuckled, their small stems all shook,
As the butterflies painted their own silly book.

So here in this plot, where chaos does reign,
The threads of each moment weave joy and some pain.
Each petal's a punchline, each leaf is a joke,
In nature's own circus, the laughter bespoke.

The Legacy of the Leaves

Once in a forest, where laughter runs free,
The leaves held a summit, sipping sweet tea.
The oak said, "I'm wise, with branches so grand!"
While the birch just snickered, "Try taking a stand!"

Each leaf had a story, a whimsy, a tune,
The maple told tales of the sun and the moon.
Hold on tight, shouted spruce, with a flick of his cap,
"We'll weather this storm, or at least take a nap!"

In the breeze, whispers of fun were exchanged,
A crabapple giggled, "My shape's been deranged!"
The pines held their breath, waiting for the punch,
As the willow did waltz, in a soft leafy crunch.

Thus, the legacy bloomed in a riotous dance,
Among shades and bright colors, each leaf found its chance.
In a tapestry woven with laughter and cheer,
Nature's own comedy blossomed right here.

Petal by Petal

Petal by petal, we giggle and sway,
The blooms are all gossiping, come what may.
The violets chuckle, with a wink and a nod,
"Did you see the bee? He forgot where he trod!"

Lilies in white wear their best flowery hats,
While poppies do pirouettes to amuse the rats.
A tulip declared, with a bright blushing hue,
"My fragrance will woo you, where's your perfume too?"

The pollen was flying, a sneeze here and there,
A sunflower blushed under the warm sunny glare.
With laughter all echoing, petals embraced,
In this garden of whimsy, we danced, we raced.

So petal by petal, we painted the scene,
With humor and fun, in colors so keen.
Nature's great laughter, a joy to behold,
A festival of blooms, with stories untold.

A Harvest of Dreams

In a field of wild wonders, where silliness blooms,
A harvest of dreams wafted sweet through the fumes.
The corn stalks were chuckling, all in a line,
As pumpkins rolled over and said, "I'm divine!"

The scarecrow was dancing, with crows on his hat,
While a rabbit hopped by, shouting, "Where are your spat?"
Turnips all tittered, just digging for gold,
"We're rootin' for laughter, as the stories unfold!"

Grapes in their bunches all toasted with cheer,
"Here's to all harvests, both far and near!"
A melon cracked jokes, in his soft juicy skin,
While carrots debated who's the best at a grin.

So gather your dreams, let your laughter take flight,
In fields of bright colors, from morning till night.
A harvest of giggles, of joy and of fun,
In this bountiful land, we all are just one.

The Blooming Path

On the road where daisies dance,
Everyone twirls in silly prance.
We stumble on petals, laughing aloud,
A garden of giggles beneath the cloud.

Bumblebees buzz with a comical hum,
As we trip on roots, oh, what a fun!
The tulips tease with their bright, bold stare,
While we chase rainbows without a care.

Sunflowers point with a wink and a grin,
Reminding us laughter is always a win.
We navigate life with blooms by our side,
In the garden of joy, come take a ride!

Beneath the Starlit Bloom

Under the glow of the moonlight fair,
We dance with the blooms, not a single care.
The roses chuckle, their thorns kept at bay,
We sway in the night; oh, what a ballet!

Lilies gossip in the soft summer breeze,
While tulips gossip with sassy degrees.
Each petal giggles as we stumble along,
In the realm of nature, we all belong.

Stars twinkle down, joining the spree,
Where daisies tease us, 'Come play with me!'
Life is a ball, filled with odd little tunes,
All beneath the starlit blooms of June.

A Bouquet of Tomorrow

With a basket of dreams, we set out to play,
Each blossom a promise, brightening the day.
A daffodil winks as we tiptoe near,
And the pansies pop up, spreading good cheer.

We gather our giggles, some daisies and sass,
In a bouquet of tomorrow, time flies by fast.
Forget-me-nots whisper, 'Stay here, don't run!'
As we tumble and trip, we're having such fun!

Every stem tells a tale, each petal a joke,
We're wrapped in the laughter that life's blooms evoke.
In the laughter of petals, we find a bright glow,
With a bouquet of moments we'll always bestow.

Tides of Fortune

On the shores where the seaweed swings,
Crabs join the party, it's always a fling.
With sea daisies dancing on the waves,
Tomorrow's fortune hidden like caves.

Jellyfish giggle, as seagulls dive down,
We wave at the blooms wearing seashells, oh clown!
The tide carries stories, both silly and brave,
As we surf through laughter, our fortunes to save.

With each splash of water, new smiles abound,
In this whimsical garden, joy is profound.
So come ride the waves, on a bright golden morn,
Where the tides of good fortune forever are born.

Gossamer Threads of Enchantment

A dandelion dared to dream,
It wished upon a sneezy gleam.
Its seeds took flight, oh what a sight,
In someone's nose, it caused a plight.

Buttercups giggled in the breeze,
As bees did dance with goofy ease.
Each bloom donned an unkempt crown,
And wore their pollen like a gown.

A tulip tried to play the part,
Of grinning joker, full of heart.
A poppy then chimed in with flair,
In laughing echoes, tossed in air.

In this garden, laughter sways,
As petals chuckle through the days.
With every rustle, joy does bloom,
Creating mischief, sweet perfume.

Echoes of the Floral Cosmos

Oh, daisies whispered in the sun,
"Who's the funniest? I bet it's none!"
Then roses blushed and joined the chat,
"Just look at me, I'm stylish, fat!"

Lilies chimed in, all prim and neat,
"What's a flower's favorite treat?"
"Petal chips with dip, I'd vote!"
While laughing leaves began to float.

Chrysanthemums laughed and shook their heads,
"Why worry 'bout the thorns in beds?"
And violets, basking in their charm,
Tickled the cacti with no alarm.

In this cosmos of bloom's delight,
Jokes of petals spark joy at night.
A garden where nothing can be sad,
Floral giggles make the heart glad.

Petals of Destiny

In a patch where daisies play,
A jester bee stole scenes today.
It buzzed a tune, oh what a sound,
As petals danced all 'round and 'round.

A sunflower wore a silly hat,
While bent low, it chattered with a cat.
"Who says we're just here to be pretty?"
Said lilac, laughing - what a witty!

The moonflower whispered, "Let's surprise!"
And brought out cookies for the skies.
With every crumb, a giggle bloomed,
In cookie crumbs, they all were groomed.

In destiny's embrace, they frolic free,
Slapstick stunts from flower to bee.
Petals laughing in an endless spree,
Nature's jesters, wild and carefree.

Whispers in the Garden

In the garden, secrets twist,
Roses whisper, "Here's a tryst!"
Marigolds snicker, "No way!"
"Let's see who can dance all day!"

The violets plotted quite the show,
With daffodils, a comical flow.
"Let's prank the bugs, give them a fright,"
A ladybug fainted, what a sight!

Tulips donned bright costumes bold,
"Who wore it best? Let's be told!"
Laughter echoed through the patch,
As blooms all giggled in a match.

In this fragrant world of glee,
Whispers bounce like bouncing bees.
A garden stage, where jokes ensue,
With nature's laughter, fresh and new.

The Seedling's Journey

In the soil, a seed did lie,
Wishing one day to touch the sky.
But oh, what a journey, full of laughs,
Hitching rides on passing cats' paths!

The roots had plans, a grand parade,
To sprout a leaf, but it delayed.
They wiggled and jiggled, played peek-a-boo,
While ants made jokes; oh yes, they knew.

A worm gave tips on wiggle-stride,
"Just keep your cool; don't let it slide!"
With sunlit hopes and rainy dreams,
This little sprout found its silly themes.

And as it grew, it waved to bees,
"Hello, my friends! Can I have some cheese?"
With laughter shared in gardens bright,
The seedling's journey felt just right.

Fragments of Sunlight

Sunbeams dance in a jolly spree,
Tickling petals of bumblebee.
"Hey, pollinate me, don't be shy!"
The daisies giggled, a floral high.

A sunspot winked, a cheeky flirt,
While roses puzzled, "Was that a skirt?"
"Oh dear, how flashy!" the tulips said,
As marigolds rolled over, giggling instead.

Chasing shadows, the bees took flight,
To swap their stories, a buzzing delight.
"Did you hear about the sunflower's craze?
It tried to nap in the sun's warm rays!"

And in the patch of cotton candy blooms,
Where each blossom giggled and consumed,
Fragments of sunlight, all around,
Laughter and joy, in nature found!

Botanical Dreams

In lands where the daisies dance and prance,
Herbs dream of winning the garden's chance.
With crowns of parsley and gowns of thyme,
They joke about cooking, oh so sublime!

A broccoli yelled, "I want to shine!"
With carrots somersaulting, feeling fine.
"Let's have a party! No veggies will lie!"
While lettuce leaf sang, "Oh me, oh my!"

Cacti joined in, with prickly cheer,
"Don't poke the fun; it's flower power here!"
Petunias played tunes on the wind's sweet breath,
Creating melodies that danced with zest.

Under the moon, they'd tell wild tales,
Of starlit dances and garden trails.
In botanical dreams, they'd frolic and scheme,
Creating a garden of joy and of gleam.

Nature's Unfolding

A tulip popped, with a cheerful grin,
"Can you believe where I have been?
Caught in a breeze, I twirled like art,
Now I stand tall, with a happy heart!"

Petals unfurl in a playful sweep,
"Who tangled my leaves? It's hard to keep!"
With sunflowers swaying, a goofy cluster,
"Just fluff and wave; let the world muster!"

A raindrop laughed as it fell from the sky,
"Splashing on daisies, oh my, oh my!"
While violets whispered, "We need a break,
Let's chill with the breeze, for goodness' sake!"

And as spring danced, with colors so bright,
The blossoms cheered, "What a splendid sight!
Through all the chuckles and giggles galore,
Nature's unfolding, forever in store!

Blossoms Before Dawn

In the garden just before light,
Petals giggle and take flight.
They dance with dew, a merry crew,
Not a care for the coming night.

Bumblebees wear tiny hats,
Chasing bugs in playful spats.
Tulips crack jokes, it's quite a show,
While daisies laugh at the rascally gnats.

Sunrise tickles every sprout,
Whispers secrets, no doubt.
But oh, the bees trip and fall,
As the laughter echoes about.

In this riot of bloom and glee,
Nature's fun is plain to see.
Each petal and stem, a jester's ploy,
In the dawn's light, wild and free.

Illuminated Meadows

In meadows bright with colors bold,
The stories of petals are happily told.
A daffodil trips, falls on its face,
As poppies chuckle, 'Well, that's quite bold!'

Butterflies play, a silly parade,
Chasing their shadows, how they invade!
Ants wearing crowns hop on their hill,
In this field of dreams, hilarity's made.

Tulips swap secrets, a gossiping spree,
While violets snicker, 'Look at me, whee!'
The breeze whispers jokes, tickling each plant,
Oh, how this meadow bursts forth with glee!

As laughter echoes in sunlit bliss,
The petals rejoice, they surely won't miss.
In this land of whimsy, where fun is the rule,
Every bloom shares a comical twist.

Fractals of Fate

In this garden where oddities sprout,
Every twist and turn fills joy with doubt.
A crocus asks, 'Where did I begin?'
While daisies respond, 'Well, that's quite a rout!'

Petals spinning in wild disarray,
Sunflowers chuckle, 'What a funny day!'
Between the rows, there's laughter and cheer,
As the roses all try to sneak away.

Jokes on the breeze as they wobble and sway,
'What's a flower's favorite game?' they say.
'Petal-to-the-metal!' they laugh as they bloom,
In a fractal dance of pure dismay.

Every twist of fate, a gag unplanned,
As blooms embrace joy, hand in hand.
They twirl through the chaos, with giggles and flair,
In this land where whimsy takes a stand.

Shades of the Unexpected

In shades of green where humor thrives,
A zany lily suddenly dives.
Roses blush, but not with shame,
As laughter spills from buzzing hives.

A tulip sneezes, the petals swirl,
The garden erupts with a giggly twirl.
'What do you call a sad buttercup?'
'A floral frown in a flowered world!'

Bumblebees play hide and seek,
Hiding beneath a giant leaf's peak.
'We'll just wait for the tickle of sun,'
'In this shade, we'll play hide and squeak!'

Each stalk has a tale, each bloom a jest,
Nature's own comedy is simply the best.
In every petal, a punchline awaits,
In this garden where joy is the quest.

The Seed of Tomorrow

In a garden of dreams, a seed took flight,
Wiggling and giggling, what a silly sight!
It danced with the raindrops, wearing a grin,
Saying, "Watch out world, here comes my kin!"

A snail passed by, with its shell so grand,
Screamed, "What a sprout! Who is this band?"
The seed just chuckled, "Oh, don't be slow,
Tomorrow I'll bloom, just you wait and see!"

The butterflies laughed, flitting nearby,
"Who knew seeds could talk? Are they all so spry?"
With a wink and a nod, the tiny seed said,
"Stick around, my friends, I won't be misled!"

Then came the sun, with a tippy-tap,
"Is it time for a party? Let's start the rap!"
So the seed wobbled, with roots all aglow,
Dancing its heart out, all agog to show!

In the Embrace of Green

In a jungle of laughter, the leaves would tease,
Whispering zingers in the soft warm breeze.
A cactus roared, "I am prickly—be warned!"
But a daisy just snickered, "Looks like you're scorned!"

As colors collided, and blooms made a fuss,
A fern flipped its fronds, saying, "Join us or bust!"
Through vines and through petals, it felt like a game,
Each flutter a giggle, no two were the same!

The sun threw a party, with rays made of cheer,
While the daisies served cookies—sweets to endear!
But the violets tall, with their heads in the clouds,
Declared, "We are royalty, all hail our crowds!"

Yet all in good fun, they danced in a line,
Grooving to nature's most hilarious rhyme.
In the embrace of green, a spectacle bright,
Where laughter and buzzing made everything right!

The Enigma of the Bloom

A bud held a secret, wrapped tight in its shell,
It giggled and hummed, a curious spell.
"Unlock me, oh world, or forever I'll pout,
For in here, I'm hiding a riddle, no doubt!"

The bees buzzed around, trying hard to guess,
"Is it chocolate? Honey? Or maybe a dress?"
But the bud just twirled, in its leafy disguise,
"You'll find out soon, just wait for the prize!"

A wise old oak chuckled, "The truth isn't far,
Maybe it's simply a bright, shining star!"
And the flowers erupted in giggles and glee,
"What if it's nothing? Just wait and see!"

At last, one fine morning, the bloom cracked wide,
Revealing a dandelion, bright and spry.
The crowd burst in laughter, the secret laid bare,
For who knew a flower could cause such a flare?

Corridor of Perfumed Paths

In a garden galore, scents wove a track,
With roses in tiaras, it was quite a knack.
The path was a puzzle of fragrance and cheer,
Where daisies would giggle, and jays flew near.

A poppy exclaimed, "Come try my cologne!
It's fresh as a breeze, from a perfume cone!"
But the marigold smirked, "Now that's a tall tale,
Mine's finer, I swear, it's bound to prevail!"

But in this wild corridor, no winner was found,
Each scent tickled noses, swirling all around.
With bees in attendance, buzzing their praise,
And the tulips all swayed in a fragrant ballet.

At dusk, as they gathered, the blooms shared a laugh,
"My essence is magic, just check out my staff!"
"Yet fragrance aside, it's the fun that we share,
In this corridor bright, perfume fills the air!"

Hope in a Blossom

In a garden bright, a sprout did rise,
With leaves like hats, oh, what a surprise!
It danced in the breeze, sang songs of glee,
Claiming, "I'm the best! Just wait and see!"

But then came the rain, a slippery slip,
It fell on its face – what a silly trip!
With muddy cheeks and a wilted grin,
It chuckled and said, "Let's try again!"

The sun peeked out, all shining and bold,
Saying, "There's magic in the laughter we hold!"
So the sprout stood tall, despite its fall,
In the garden of dreams where fun reigns over all.

With pollen pretzels and nectar tea,
It threw a party – come one, come three!
So remember this tale of the sprout so bright,
Even if you fall, you've got to delight!

A Spectrum of Potential

A little bud whispered, "I want to be,
A rainbow of colors, as bright as can be!"
From purple to pink, from yellow to blue,
It asked all the bees, "What should I do?"

The bees buzzed loudly, "Just wait and see,
You'll bloom in the sunlight, just trust in glee!"
But the bud was impatient, it started to pout,
"Why can't I be stunning? I want to stand out!"

Then one early morn, with a blink and a stretch,
It burst into bloom, like a startling sketch!
"Look at me! Look at me! I'm a sight to behold,
A spectrum of colors, I'm bold and I'm gold!"

But wait! There's a twist that you might not expect,
The pot was too small, what a bizarre neglect!
It giggled and whispered, "Well, I'll just grow wide,
For the world is my canvas; I'll open quite wide!"

The Flower that Wasn't

In a patch of green, there thrived a weed,
With dreams of being fancy, a delicate seed.
It donned a big hat, with ruffles and flair,
Saying, "Call me Flora, if you dare!"

But Flora, alas, was a bit too confused,
For she often forgot her style was misused.
Each time she strut with a wiggle and shake,
Neighbors all chuckled, "She's just a mistake!"

With petals of fuzz, she tickled the air,
And claimed, "My dear friends, don't you dare stare!"
Yet deep down inside, Flora did know,
That even a weed could put on a show.

As seasons changed, in her heart she found,
True beauty is joy, let laughter abound!
So she spread her charm, let everyone see,
That being unique is just simply glee!

Radiance in the Shadows

In the corner of gloom, a daisy declared,
"Though the sun's not around, you're still unprepared!"
With a wink to the moon and a jig on the floor,
She shouted, "I'm fabulous! Who needs the sun's score?"

Her petals were bright, like a lamp in the night,
"Just dance in the dark; it will all be alright!"
The stars were her friends, twinkling with joy,
As the shadows embraced her, a radiant ploy.

With laughter and giggles, she stole the show,
"In darkness I thrive; oh, look at me glow!"
The night critters laughed, few held in despair,
For the daisy proved fun was found everywhere!

So if you feel dim, in your own private shade,
Just channel your sparkle, don't let it fade!
For the magic of life can bloom in the night,
When you find joys small, you'll shine ever bright!

The Aroma of Anomalies

On a hilltop, scents run wild,
Barking dogs and cows beguiled.
A rose leaned in for a cheesy chat,
While daisies danced like they were flat.

The sun wore shades, sipping tall drinks,
A lily whispered, 'We've got some kinks!'
Bees started dancing, what a sight,
A bumbling bug lost its flight.

With every whiff, the world gets strange,
A tulip giggles, 'What's the change?'
Each petal hides a quirky joke,
In gardens where the weeds just smoke.

So here we laugh at nature's play,
With fragrant friends who love to stray.
When smells collide, the fun's in store,
An aromatic world we can't ignore.

Dreams in the Wild

In fields of green, the dreams collide,
A dandelion starts to slide.
It tickles bees, says, 'Catch me soon!'
While poppies sing a silly tune.

A quirky fern tells tales of glee,
Of grass that danced and drank sweet tea.
With butterflies in top hats prancing,
They twirl around, it's quite enhancing.

A rosebud snoozes, snoring fun,
While daisies argue, who's number one.
They trade silly puns like it's a game,
In dreams where no one feels the shame.

So grab a crown of petals bright,
Join wild dreams that take to flight.
In laughter and love, we all belong,
In this silly world, we can't go wrong.

A Patchwork of Daisies

In a patchwork quilt of colors wide,
Daisies seem to take a stride.
They wear polka dots and stripes galore,
While giggling softly, 'We want more!'

The daisies conspire, with laughter bold,
Planning a prank that's never old.
A gopher wanders, thinks he's so sly,
While petals whisper, 'Oh, he'll pry!'

They giggle whenever the sun peeks in,
That golds the rogue who thinks he can win.
They twirl and swirl in a sunny lay,
With secrets tucked in their flowery sway.

With each little breeze, mischief's afoot,
A patchwork tale where fun is put.
In fields of whimsy, let's all partake,
With daisies laughing, for goodness' sake!

Serendipitous Sprouts

In the garden, sproutlings appear,
Wobbling 'round, consuming cheer.
They didn't plan on sprouting so bright,
But now they're making quite the sight!

A sunflower claims it's the tallest around,
While lilypads giggle at their silly sound.
With roots that dance and leaves that sway,
Each plant's got a joke for the lovely day.

The tulips twist and show some flair,
Chasing butterflies without a care.
A patch of carrots shimmies and shakes,
Wishing they were cakes for heaven's sakes!

So as serendipity blooms away,
In this botanical cabaret,
Join the frolic, give in to fun,
For every sprout has just begun!

Echoing Blossom

In a garden not too far,
The daisies sing bizarre.
They whisper jokes to the breeze,
Tickle the petals with ease.

Sunflowers wear a funny hat,
Laughing at a lazy cat.
The roses giggle and sway,
Chasing their worries away.

Bees buzz with a comedic flair,
Spreading pollen everywhere.
Even the grass has a grin,
As they dance with the din.

A tulip took a selfie shot,
What a funny little plot!
And in this whimsical space,
Life's a riot—what a race!

Dancing with Dandelions

Dandelions in a row,
Wiggle like they know.
They chuckle in the wind's sway,
Planning their mischief play.

One sends fluff to a friend,
'Catch me if you can,' they send!
Round and round they go with glee,
In a puffy jubilee.

Butterflies join in the frolic,
Strutting, never melancholic.
They trade jokes while sipping dew,
In this garden, laughter grew.

Every petal a story told,
In shades of yellow and gold.
Jokes and giggles fill the air,
Dancing without a single care!

The Garden of What Could Be

In a patch where wishes bloom,
Each thought dispels the gloom.
A band of daisies joked 'Why not?'
Plan your dreams, don't be caught.

A vine twists in a silly knot,
Saying, 'I'm the tightest spot!'
But the lilies roll with cheer,
'Just let loose—we're all here!'

A thoughtful willow leans low,
'What if we went with the flow?'
Frayed edges laugh with pride,
In this wacky plant-filled ride.

Cosmic giggles come alive,
In the place where wishes thrive.
The snickers burst—charming and free,
In the garden of what could be!

Petals and Possibilities

Petals tumble, flip, and spin,
Joining in the laughter din.
Every hue, a jest, a pun,
Sunshine grins—oh what fun!

Lilacs blush in shades of glee,
Trading jokes with bumblebees.
Each ray of light—sparkling bright,
Dancing in sheer delight.

Tulips try to tell a tale,
Of a snail who set his sail.
'Onward!' he exclaimed with flair,
Found a flower—loved the air!

While petals swirl with hopes anew,
They find the funny in the blue.
Each moment a joyful spree,
In petals and possibilities!

Unexpected Blooms

In a garden full of socks,
A daisy wore a pair of crocs.
The bees all laughed, what a sight!
Dancing blooms in sheer delight.

A rose with shades of bubblegum,
Swayed along to a silly drum.
Its petals twinkled like a star,
Inviting all the critters near and far.

The daisies held a tea party,
With ants in hats, oh so hearty!
They sipped on dew from tiny cups,
And shared bad puns with giggles and ups.

Then came a storm, rain fell like glee,
The blooms all bounced just like a spree.
They twirled in puddles, oh what fun!
A floral party under the sun!

The Allure of Green

A cactus wore a funny grin,
Spouting jokes while sipping gin.
It tickled all the leaves around,
With puns that made the grass astound.

Tulips thought they were so grand,
Bowing low to make a stand.
But every gust of wind that blew,
Had them tumbling, oh who knew?

A lettuce leaf in disco shoes,
Thought it could dance to those old blues.
But every twist made heads collide,
And soon it was a wild ride!

The ferns just laughed, they leaned in tight,
As petunias tried to hold on right.
In shades of green, they all took part,
In a blooming jest that warmed the heart!

Trails of the Blossoming

A wandering bloom with cap and cane,
Set off to seek some sweet champagne.
With every step, it tripped and fell,
Crying, 'Oh why must I rebel!'

The violets played a tag of chase,
Winding through their flowered space.
But oh, the bees were quite a sight,
Buzzing in circles, taking flight.

A dandelion spun fast and round,
Feeling quite like royalty crowned.
It sneezed so loud, the garden shook,
As petals scattered like a book!

And in the end, with laughter loud,
They formed a wild and happy crowd.
Each bloom agreed, through silly quests,
Life's strange wit is what they loved best!

The Gathering of Wishes

A sunflower held a carnival fair,
With popcorn blooms and petals to share.
The daisies juggled while marigolds spun,
Cheering for all, oh wasn't it fun?

A wishbone branch began to play,
Strumming tunes on a cloudy day.
Butterflies danced in elegant twirls,
While pansies giggled, wearing pearls.

The tulips ran a fortune booth,
Telling tales, uncovering truth.
But when a bee buzzed into the scene,
The fortunes flew off, oh what a routine!

At dusk, they gathered, sharing a cheer,
For whimsical thoughts that danced in the ear.
From dreams and chuckles, they all knew,
Each wish made here would surely come true!

www.ingramcontent.com/pod-product-compliance
Lightning Source LLC
Chambersburg PA
CBHW071814160426
43209CB00003B/85